Book of One :-)

Volume 3

Lightworker's Log

SAM

This book is dedicated to those "walking their talk" to be examples of the Christ Consciousness that continues to blossom within humanity.

Contents

Part Two: Author's Experiences

Preface

Never in my wildest dreams did I ever consider the life I now lead. It was totally unheard of to envision channeling words from higher realms ten years ago but now it's become rather common. As this volume goes to press, I now look forward to sensing and documenting messages from other realms of this illusion, for yes, all life on earth is but a figment of imagination. Keep this in mind as we move further down the rabbit hole!

Shine on :-)

SAM
Summer 2014
Fort Lauderdale, Florida

~ Part One ~
Volume 3

A New Illusion

"You are beginning to realize that everything in this world is illusion. That being said, be aware of your thoughts for they build this illusion to your liking. You cannot exist in this illusion without building it with thought so be sure to monitor your thoughts consciously.

"Build your world with life-affirming and healthy thoughts. Do not feed those thoughts of limitation or unwholeness, for that is what you will experience. Be aware that all on this earth hold this power to build the perfect Nirvana and mold your world carefully.

"We are the Keeper of One here to help those ready to move forward to a new illusion."

"I AM the perfection of *All That Is*, in perfect form, building the New World."

೮ 📖 ೞ

Acceptable Reality

"An acceptable reality is where all are living in Abundance, free to relish in Oneness. An acceptable reality is one where all are free to be Whole in every way. An acceptable reality is one where each unit of the Whole is free to contribute to the richness of *All That Is* without any limitation whatsoever. An acceptable reality is one where all are free to choose greater ways of living, greater ways of loving, greater ways of BEing. Choose your acceptable reality and know it is within your reach.

"That is what we came to relate at this time. You do not live in an acceptable reality because you are not aware of the choices. Be aware of the vast choices of health, wealth, and wholeness in all things. Be aware of the life affirming ways to live and know you are on the cusp of this reality now.

"We are the Keeper of One coming through the channel as agreed to before birth."

₧ 📖 ₧

Adrenal Workout

"The adrenals are getting a workout, so to speak, from the DNA change within. You will find that this passes in time. But for the meantime, you may increase your intake of selenium and watch the fluoride intake as suspected. It is for a number of years that this change takes place and you are but one of many undergoing the process.

"You must adhere fully to your own resonance and go within whenever experiencing physical symptoms. Seek medical help as necessary when you cannot find relief through alternative methods. We are watching as you go through this process and will guide as necessary to keep you as whole as possible. Seek not outside your Self of One."

ೞ 📖 ೦ʒ

Advancing is the Name of the Game

"Earth's star is a fully polarized system of Light.

"Advancing is the name of the game as these new energies pummel earth unceasingly. Times have never been clearer, times of reaping the Oneness of *All That Is* for all of humanity. Seek not to displeasure the Self of One for it lives within you glowing brightly as these energies assimilate easily and gracefully within you. Pay no heed to the soothsayers as they continue to grasp the old ways. These ways are quickly dissipating with the Light that pummels the earth of One.

"Seemingly contractual obligations exist no more as these old systems fall away. Bear nothing here but the Light of One for that is the light that you are.

"Nothing is lost. Nothing is gained. Remember, all here is illusion.

"All here on this plane are aware of the changes taking place if even subconsciously. All know this is the greatest time of humanities progression towards the evolution of the physical form. Those wishing to keep their forms as they are shall no longer be supported on this earth.

"There is much work to be done for the lightworkers. Each knowingly comes forth, even if unknowingly, knowing the truth of their tasks. All will soon relish in these energies wholly and completely. The forbearers go before the others to assimilate these energies and show that it can be done. The Truth responds

4

in kind as all see the changes these forbearers bring about within your world of One.

"On the cusp of sleep the portal sits, the portal to the dimensions you seek. Higher energies exist within these dimensions. And in continuing into them, your body must change. Therefore, this is the reason these energies come to you now, through the earth, the very earth on which you live. As it changes, the body's magnetics change as well. And these magnetics allow you to connect to these higher dimensions. These dimensions are more in tune to the crystalline structure your body now morphs into."

೫ 📖 ೞ

All That Is Guides

"Thou art that of which *It* is. There is never reason to fear, to ponder over future illusions, for the *All That Is* within guides every moment of life."

୨୦ 📖 ଓଗ

Be Mindful

"Your family's well-being lies with you. Send them, and all living things, the Light and Love of One, whenever you can, as these gross energies on earth compete with the Light and Love of I AM. It is in your power to change the world in which you live with your thoughts, your deeds, your dreams of Wholeness and Truth. Be ever mindful of these habitual ways of being as all things fall away to be replaced with new."

ॐ 📖 ☙

Brothers and Sisters of Light Speak

"Words are so grossly overrated but it is all we have at this point in time and space to reach through the veil of illusion. It is, after all, in the feeling, the sixth sense if you will, that the real story of your BEing is unfolding. Take time to feel this sixth sense as part of the Whole of *All That Is* for in coming days it will be most welcome to escape the 3-D reality you have made for yourself.

"As new things fall into place, old institutions will waver and fall. This is the message we relate today. Your world changes vastly in this your year 2014, more than ever before, as old safety nets are wiped away by the few who think they rule the world. This time shall not last long but will be gruesome for many. You must follow your instincts to remain out of the fray of the disillusioned. Keep thoughts pure and simple, upon a simpler way of living and you shall be fine as these necessary changes take place. All is ultimately well in this world that now changes beyond recognition. Find your faith in the *Source of I AM* and know you are not alone in the journey.

"We are your brothers and sisters of Light ready to assist all those wavering along the evolutionary path."

℘ 📖 ℘

Call to Oneness

"The call to Oneness increases steadily as all fall prey to energies of a human nature. Let not these appearances of separation alarm or cause thoughts other than Oneness. The task of all lightworkers is to now spread the Word of One, the only Truth that exists. For it is a whisper away from your physical reality.

"As things unfold in your physical world, let not the mines of separation draw you into another dimensional reality, for all are now called to step-up, so to speak, to greater awareness of the Self within. Choose thoughts carefully as you motor along the Oneness path for each though spurs forth its subsequent reality in your word.

"Do not be deceived into thinking you alone bear the Light of One but know each, in its own time, comes forth to spread the Light of Oneness that humanity seems to have forgotten. Each human has its own time of awakening. Be aware that many chose not to awaken at this monumental time in humanity's history.

"Let all things pass, as you remain aware of True Self, always bearing a demeanor of non-reaction. Each reaction causes a subsequent manifestation so be aware of thoughts on a daily basis."

❧ 📖 ☙

Chaos and Self

"As you work forward to the bonding of Self, in small mind, know that we are with you, paving the way to your own greatness, for each I AM Presence abides within a state of pure grace and wonder that only you can imagine through your own efforts. Know that as things fall into place in your world, the chaos outside you is yet another signal of the desire to find the Self, the Self most unerringly toward the greatness of I AM. The I AM Presence assures the wholeness of all."

       80 📖 ca

Communicate

"We are taking on new forms to relish in the Oneness of Love and Light once again. Be sure to take the time to reconnect with that part of yourself that wishes to communicate. It is, after all, a part of you long forgotten but nevertheless ready to return to full consciousness.

"Take the time to change habits of old for newer ones of higher energies as your world continues to change. Be ever mindful of the world's illusionary, deceitful ways to get you out of your True Self and into thoughts not life affirming. Beware of those speaking of separation, and fear not in coming days as all things change quickly to an unrecognizable state for many. Those who follow the Light and Love of Oneness are carefully watched. It is not a ploy of separation but a knowing of your true nature that allows this to occur. All are watched carefully yet some choose not to follow the path of Oneness. In the grand scheme of things, this too is fine, as all is ultimately illusion on your earth. Let the games continue as you choose your own path and be sure that the path you choose is appropriate for you.

"I am yet another aspect of the great Whole, here to communicate with all who ask me to do so. Again, there is no name for me but you can refer to me as the Lightness of Love and True BEing."

ॐ 📖 ॐ

Community Increases Awareness

"You are moving into the realm of increased awareness as all community forms to re-connect. Let your days and nights be filled with the treasures of full life as each shares their own journey of awareness.

"The days before you change with fervor (intensity) to maintain the status quo. Those of you purging and cleansing will pave a new path for others to follow when the time is right for them. Each one has their own time to return to full awareness. Let this not affect your path but maintain steady progress toward the BEingness of *All That Is.* "Remember to pay close attention to all that enters your field of awareness for much is yet to be cleared and cleansed before you can come into full awakening.

"I bid you farewell on this day of great progress for humanity. I am the Keeper of One."

ଚ୍ଚ 📖 ଓ

Connect with Self

"In the silence comes the twilight of remembering. To fully remember your True BEing, you must now take that time to go within. It is, after all, an aspect you have long forgotten, left behind in the fray of new experience, new adventures of illusion. Take this time in the early dawn hours, or near the end of day at dusk, to reap the best benefit of remembering and connecting with lost aspects of your Self."

ಹಿ 📖 ಣ

Drink from the Loving Cup of Life

"Drink from the loving cup of Life as you enter this New World of Love and Light. Those of humanity now ready, move forward to fulfill their soul work knowing all is as it was and shall be forevermore as the rest of humanity lives in the past. Continue to move forward as you bear the Light of One for *All*. Let nothing dissuade you from achieving the glory of your true BEing.

"I am Sanat Kumara here to guide all who chose to ascend with Mother Earth."

ಽಂ 📖 ೞ

Earth Systems Change

"Disclosure of all warped earth systems is near as unseen forces move closer to your reality. Your bubble of biology bursts forth to reveal unheard of heights of awareness very soon. As these great changes take place, remember to guard thoughts carefully.

"All earth systems now change at an unheard of rate of growth as you move closer to the Nirvana of BEing. Take all things in stride and know the immense changes before you are but a glimmer of what is to come. When you step into that aspect of BEing that holds only thoughts of Oneness, you know you have arrived at that perfect state of Nirvana. Many more in humanity will feel this wondrous sense of Oneness very soon.

"You are at the cusp of a new awakening for humanity as all lie in readiness to step into the New World. This world is yours for the asking, if only in mind for many who fail to seek the safety and security of Oneness, the Wholeness of Self that never left. Bear witness to the New World as those not yet ready to step forward fall further into limitation and fear. This avenue is yet but another more strenuous way to reach Wholeness of Self. For all come to earth to experience what is needed to play the game of human life fully.

"Reap not in sorrow nor in haste as this old world crumbles before your eyes. You alone hold the power to reap in Wholeness and Truth the BEingness you came to experience as a soul. Let not the vast changes of earth affect you detrimentally but know all aspects must play out to reach the Nirvana humanity now strives to exist within.

଼ 📖 ଓ

Edging toward True Unity

"Blessings be upon you now as we skirt through this process of galactic cooperation. Your earth ways spin out of control as we watch from other realms lending support to those asking for assistance. We are never far from the thoughts of those ready to recognize our unity as a Whole.

"Be ever mindful of your willingness to seek assistance from higher realms and know we are parts of you yet unrecognized by many figments of imagination. All lie in readiness to come forth when the time allows true Unity of BEing.

"We are the Galactic Federation of Light"

∞ 📖 ∞

Examine Emotions

"Ego speaks for you at many times when you remain unaware. Hone your ability to tap-in by paying attention to emotions for they are key to this matrix of belief. You must motor through this maze effortlessly to help others do the same and it is truly the emotions that guide the way though. Let us help you motor through the maze by listening to those messages, by paying attention to synchronicities and being ever present in your body.

"Your body speaks to you throughout the day. Take the time to listen. In the event of each ache and pain take the time to examine your thoughts and feelings at the time. To rid your self of these occurrences, it is as easy as recognizing the feeling, feeling it fully and allowing it to work though the body system before allowing it to dissipate into the nothingness from whence it came.

"You are on the cusp of greatness of Selfhood, meaning you are awakening fully to the Christ Consciousness where there is no disease, no separation from thoughts, feelings, people or responses to what many consider outside themselves. It is of the utmost concern that you recognize the severity of your responses to each occurrence, situation that arises. For your responses will always define your outcomes. Take this message with the resonance ability that you have to decipher the truth and know we are with you ever ready to show the way to true BEingness of Self.

We are the White-Winged Consciousness of Nine."

క్ర 📖 ౮

Expanding the Spark Within

"The time is coming when all shall expand into the Light of One. This is a new game for humanity in as much as it has never been played on any realm. Stay clear in your thinking to play it. And know that you are one of many who chose this experience.

"No nurturing task can provide more wonder than that within. It is time for humanity to bring forth that which lies within. The spark of Oneness lies within ready for all to ignite."

୫୦ 📖 ୧ଓ

Experience, Express and Expand

"The beautiful Light of I AM is everywhere. This presence awaits your recognition as all move closer in consciousness to *All That Is*.

"Life is an experience. We each have our own lane, so to speak, and conditions, which we choose through our free will. Use your free will wisely to experience, express and expand!"

❧ 📖 ☙

Forging into the New World

"The days shall be gruesome at best but you shall overcome them using the Power of One. There is much to be done in your world as this great shift takes place. Know you are one of many who will forge ahead into another world while those left behind in the fray of forgetting remain in dire circumstances. It is their choice to remain and experience certain aspects of being not yet fully experienced by their soul.

You shall, as many others, lead the masses of false consciousness to higher ground, so to speak, higher states of awareness, through your work of One. Each soul now has the choice to move through the gateway of Light. This choice is always there, regardless of creed, race, or origin. Do not be distracted by what seems to go on around you but pay attention to only your thought process. Make sure to relinquish those thoughts not in tune with the Oneness of *All That Is*. This is a necessary step to lead all toward the fullness of BEing.

"Take care in the days ahead and know, that of what it Is is within you to pave the way to greatness. There is no other way to relish in the Oneness but to relinquish the bonds of separation and trade them into the bonds of Oneness, Beauty, Love, Light and *All the Good There Is*.

"I am the Keeper of One here to help you and others forge ahead into the New World."

෨ 📖 ෬

Game Changers

"To travel along this path wholly, you must adhere to the rules of the game. This game changes with each thrust of Mother Earth's movement. It begins to change with each thought and deed of those upon her. As things continue to change at an alarming rate, those of you who know the rules of the game (Thought makes your world; Oneness is the Key; Love is all there truly is.) will play the game as masters, living in the moment of Now with no regrets or unnecessary disadvantages.

"The higher realms are with you as you move through this process of returning to Source. Let nothing dissuade you from this process of returning for all will eventually do so in a short period of time left on your earth. As the ethers of change are upon you, move into them with the fluidly and grace of a master, letting go of old beliefs, old habits, old ways of living and being, to take on new greater ways of expressing and living in the New World of Love and Light. You are on the precipice of change as all march forward into the unknown. It is the great pleasure of your soul to move through this process, in this life, as many others watch from other realms of illusory existence.

I am the Keeper of One here to guide, to watch over those ready to move into this New World of Love and Light with grace and ease."

℘ 📖 ⱽ

Greater Opportunities

"I AM one with the Power and the Wisdom to draw forth unknown realities into this world. I do so now with the help of my unseen entourage that is ever near and ready to assist in the awakening of my soul's work. The soul's work is now of utmost concern as this realm of illusion moves further into chaos. It is my soul's charge to change the course of events to one of more liking.

"I draw forth into this illusion greater opportunities for myself and all humankind."

ଛ 📖 ଔ

It is a Feeling My Dear!

"One need only ask for direction to receive it. After all, it is your higher aspect, so to speak for lack of a more appropriate word, that does the directing. Let me put that another way, other aspects of your soul are ready and waiting to be recognized as part of the illusion in which you live. All is well as you incorporate greater aspects of each part of your figment, the figment of *All That Is*.

"As you incorporate these aspects, you shall experience greater periods of multi-dimensionality, more times spent in other parts of the illusion matrix. This is a necessary course of events for all aspects to coalesce before dissipating back to the grandness of *All That Is*. And yet, you know in the deep recesses of soul that even you are illusion. But as told throughout time, each figment, as you call yourself, must join with all others to return in entirety.

"Your very BEing is not on any realm of illusion but housed within the glory and wholeness of *All That Is*. This is an unbroken state of ecstasy and Love, untouched. You shall again experience this aspect of your BEing when time and space dissipate into the grandness of Self love at all times. Each soul has its own journey but each is a part of the other so remember to re-member as you move through the matrix of time and space.

"I am yet another aspect of your soul, ready and able to assist from other periods and spaces of the illusion. We have no names on this level of illusion but you may refer to me as the wind and sunshine of time well spent. It is a feeling my dear."

જ 📖 ଔ

Journey to Light

"There is a greater awareness in every cell of your body as these portals of awareness open. Be aware of these times as ones of great necessity to carry you through the portals to a greater awareness and understanding of Self, of the I AM Presence within.

"As your world continues to change you shall expect these sessions of Light building on a greater level. They shall help you to move with Mother Earth when the time is right. All on your planet do not experience these changes to the extent as others. But you must move forward in your awareness, keeping these changes to yourself, for not all understand the process, or even the ability to forgo it.

"We are the Keeper of One in unique form, as you, but on other realms of the illusion. There is no time nor space where we exist. It is a place you will experience in your journey to Light as well."

80 📖 03

Limiting Beliefs

"You are on a path of full awakening. Stay clear of the fray of old beliefs. Those not yet ready to travel the path of One, the path of awaking to True Self, shall remain in the fray of old limiting beliefs. That is the message we offer on this Memorial Day weekend in your world."

ॐ 📖 ☙

Living in the Light of One

"The time is ripe. The hour is here. Your delivery is at hand. Be sure to focus on the positive aspects of life as you motor through your day. Each thought builds on some level of reality so be sure to manifest those thoughts you wish to improve your life and world. Know that all things change in your world as denser, darker energies dissipate. The world before you now spins out of control and yet it offers a new way of being, a way where all come together to live in the Light of One.

"The task before the lightworkers are assurety of the path they travel. Unique, vibrant voices fill the earth with their glory. We all see the need for bright ions of Light to fill this world with Oneness. It is up to you to set your mind at ease. If repeating affirmations works do that but know all is quite well on the other side of knowing. The richness not yet expressed in your world is already expressed on other realms. One needs only to recognize the Truth of Reality to express that richness in your own reality."

ஒ 📖 ௸

Massive Waves Cause Changes

"Love and compassion produced by the masses causes a wave of Truth over earth. As this massive wave of Truth covers your earth, be prepared for new beginnings. Many lightworkers not yet in place, for what is to come, will now meet their destiny in places not visited before. Know that your role as a maker of Peace and Truth is within yourself even though it seems apart from the physicality.

"As this massive wave of the greatest Love ever felt on earth continues to implode, know that many others are prepared to move on in other ways. More souls than ever before now leave to play their game elsewhere. This, now, is a new beginning for those not yet ready to forgo the human ways participated in for eons.

"Be it known that all change now occurring on earth is not foretold but relished as a new game to play for those ready to make Heaven on earth. This Heaven breaks forth in eruptions unheard of and unexpected as humanity continues to cause positive changes through its efforts for Peace and greater Love.

"All is well for those participating in these efforts. Fear not as we move closer to the Nirvana never experienced on any plane, at any time in your field of space."

৪০ 📖 ৫৪

Maze of Illusion

"All is well on this grand earth ride you now find yourself upon. Take these days easily and stay within your heart of hearts, the true place of your BEing.

"Each person, each circumstance, each journey you take is meant to help you purge old beliefs of limitation. You now move forward in this journey of Light to muse those ready to move forward. It is with this time that each moves more quickly upon the Path of Light to become more readily available to those seeking disclosure, seeking new areas of their lives to cleanse. It is with this forward move in thinking that you become aware of the need to stay within the heart of the small one.

"We are the Keeper of One, ever-ready to serve those parts of yourself still lost in the maze of illusion."

℥ 📖 ℣

Message on Morphing

"The concentration of today's energies is intense as you move through this process of clearing and cleansing. Be aware that not all have chosen to forgo this monumental change at this time. Keep remarks and notes of the process to your small self of one for those going through the process as well. Do not share your journey with those unaware of these changes for it merely serves to confuse them.

"Know that many of you now move forward on the path of ascension (changing awareness of Oneness) much faster than others. Be sure to keep the process pure, by remaining within your own system of thought and action, and know you are carefully guided and watched over as these changes occur to help humanity."

ꝏ 📖 ꝏ

Moving Closer in Form

"Come forth and behold the glory of your physical form as it morphs closer to the Reality of *All That Is*. This occurrence has, as yet, never been seen on any realm of existence. But humanity agreed to this pleasure of BEing in a state of readiness to explore the options of morphing back to a form left eons ago.

"As many of you move closer to this reality be aware that others chose not to experience the morphing in this human lifetime. There shall, despite many naysayers, be other opportunities to bear the Light of One for them, for change is but a whisper away for those who wish.

"All is not, as you say, above board, for those on earth. For many now relish in the darkness of deceit and lies, which shall be disclosed very shortly. Make no noise upon this earth unless it is harmonious with the truer aspects of *All That Is*. Know that all lies in readiness to forge ahead into this unknown land of reality as much of humanity sleeps, while others morph closer to the true form left long ago."

༂ 📖 ༃

Nothing Remains

"As you move further into the Land of Oz, the way of Love is key. This means to follow your heart in all circumstances. This may not be easy for some as conditions radically change. Pay attention to your thoughts as these times become a struggle for many in your world. Do not enter the land of limitation with them (through thoughts or otherwise) but center yourself in Love, move into your heart space, and know all is in Divine Order.

"Your world now moves further toward the Light and Love it once was as these changes take place. Nothing, alas, in your world remains the same.

"I am the Keeper of One here to help all who ask for assistance."

ജ 📖 ങ

Portals to a New Era

"You are called upon to witness the changing of the guard. The silence now experienced will soon break out into a crescendo of Peace, of Love, of Harmony for all humankind as the witnesses around the earth and beyond spread the Light of Oneness. Your earth now moves into a New Era, never experienced on any realm, in any time or space, as all watch.

"To enter the portals more fully remember, thoughts make your world. Concentrate on those life-affirming thoughts of Love, Peace, Joy and Abundance for all. Those are the things to manifest more freely in your world as these necessary changes take place.

"Beware of those thoughts decreasing the vibrational rate and push them aside to nurture your Lightbody. Yes, feel your feelings but do not concentrate on them or claim them. Consider what you wish to experience and concentrate on that instead."

஫ 📖 ௐ

Reality

"You are awaking to the true reality of Home. In this Reality, you will find that things come to you easily. Others may not experience this so be careful with your words and keep much to yourself. As this separation, only in experience, unfolds for those in the Light of One, you may be confronted with gross earth disturbances. Do not let these disturb you but remain heart centered, for each soul chose their experiences on earth before birth. Know that as things change in your world, the Home you exist in remains the same."

"We are the Keeper of One, many forms of essence, in one body of knowledge and Truth."

80 📖 ∞

Reality Changes

"Yes, the mental burdens are beginning to lift. You will find that those still lost in the maze of drama and confusion do not wish to change their ways. This is the final break from 3-D reality.

"For those wishing to move forward, know that many in your world will no longer relate to your abundance, happiness, and peace. This is as it should be for recall; all souls choose their own experience.

"More changes are to come but for those immersed in the path of Oneness all is quite well. Continue to bear the Light of One. Spread that Light at will throughout your neighborhoods to receive the full blessing of what is to come.

"Those of you who embark on this journey of Love and Kindness know full well what lies ahead for those that do not. But all is ultimately well, for your world is but an illusion lost in the mind of small ones, still not ready to seek the Wholeness and Purity of One."

૪૦ 📖 ઝ

Rules to the Game

"You are in a space of consciousness where all is known and yet held back by the little ego, the small self of one. It is not the first time this has occurred in your lives but this time you shall break through the barrier of silence, or dare we say, over-thought, to reap the pleasures of full BEing, yes, in this life, in this body you call yours.

"Remain in the throe of questions and you shall remain in the sense of a body. This is the cherished place for ego to be. But what if you just continued on to live in the moment of Now, the only true moment where time does not exist? We tell you that is the way to live. It is the way of the masters of old and it will become your way, more so with each passing day.

"Have nothing hold you back. Yes, feel the feelings as they rise but do not dwell upon them or they keep the mind-body thought system ever thinking, out of the present moment. The key to your daily trials and tribulations is to be conscious of living in a world where all is not as it seems and yet play by the rules. Do you understand this? You must pay attention to the rules of the game that keep all bound by limited conditions, those that affect your own way of being, and take care to avoid unnecessary trauma.

"Remember to make the most of each moment. Do not hold back for fear of not fitting in. Do not go forth without being aware of the consequences in a world where all is illusion and yet play the game well, mastering all situations with ease and grace, taking responsibility for every thought, word, deed of life."

৪০ 📖 ৩

Secure Your Place

"The time is coming when all shall see the glory of the god within. Speak not in sorrow, nor in haste, but know all things spoken reveal the truth within. Your world changes quickly as all on other realms of BEing watch.

"You are living the thoughts of many others as you go about your day. Be assured this time will not last long as the last vestiges of old purge and cleanse. This time is unknown on your earth. And yet it is indeed a necessary and prophetic time. For all now live within the bounds of Oneness and Love regardless of their propensities to hang onto old ways.

"Take the time needed to rest and secure your place in the New World as all things old fall away."

ॐ 📖 ೞ

Seed Group Message

"Remember areas of interest as you go through this process. They are the ones to bring humanity back to Wholeness, starting with you.

- "Keep thoughts pure – no separation, no negativity, etc.

- "Hone the Lightbody – move Light through the physical frame.

- "Avoid the chaos – do not pay attention to mass media but look within for pertinent news.

- "Feed the physical frame with nurturing food and drink – fresh fruit, vegetables, pure water, etc.

- "Exercise to keep in shape as the body continues to morph – walk through your neighborhoods spreading Love and Light.

- "Seek not outside yourself for sustenance.

"Know that humanity now moves though the process of clearing and cleansing. Many will attempt to lay blame upon others to avoid this. Know that you alone carry the Power of Wholeness for each carries their own weight. Issues cannot be placed upon others but must be cleared and cleansed individually by looking upon the Christ Seed within. As the clearing/cleansing process accelerates, know that all is ultimately well for as souls you chose to move through this process successfully.

"Remember, all things on earth are ultimately illusion. Yet each soul must return to the Wholeness of its True Self to play the game of experience, expression, and expansion on other realms.

"I bid you good day. I am Amanda, a part of the seed group for humanity come to right misperceptions."

හ 📖 ශ

Self-Identity

"The only thing to escape from is your mind. Self-identity, what do you identify with? Do you identify with a body or a spirit experiencing itself in human form? Those are the questions to ask yourself to go beyond this temporal illusion of space and time. Those are the questions that can and will set you free of all dis-ease, all limitation, all discordant energies. You must trust your Self to shine through during this period of mass upheaval on your earth.

"Once again, nothing remains the same. Trust your inner guidance to carry you through these times with ease and grace. Go within and seek nothing outside your Self.
"We are the Keeper of One."

ಏ 📖 ಚ

Separation is Over

"Be it known on all levels of reality, the days and nights, the very times, of separation are over. Although you may seem to exist in time and space, it is yet another false representation of the True Self of One. This Oneness is *All There Is* and ever shall be, disguised in many different representations to express the richness not yet realized by its very figments.

"As you move further into this process of knowing, on all levels of creation, the true expansion of Self, remember to go with the flow and allow the flow to move through you with ease and grace.

"We are yet in form but need not stress that separate part of BEingness as such. The actions to take are now of solidarity and Oneness in all aspects for as you reap so shall you sow. Recognize each person you meet in your earthly sojourns as yet another aspect of yourself waiting for recognition, waiting for the love it so richly deserves. And know you are yet another aspect of the richness of all BEing, condensed into a solid form for greater expression and purpose than realized.

"We are the Galactic Federation of Light, yet another aspect of *All There Is*, on yet another realm of existence expressing the Source of *All.*"

৪০ 📖 ෙ

Shine the Light Of One

"When we continue to walk upon the waters of contentment, those who do not see our Light. Let the Light of One shine forth as humanity goes through this purging and cleansing. Know that all is not as it seems, for unseen forces manipulate the masses of what many would call evil, to bear the fruits of Oneness, never to separate in form again. Your brothers and sisters of Light will assure that those who wish harm and separation do not fulfill their goals.

"Remember, energy flows where attention goes. Focus only on the Love and Light of your I AM Presence to weather this storm."

ᖇ 📖 ᘓ

Sleeping Habits

"Sleeping habits may change. Do not concern yourself with this course of events if you are able to rest as desired/needed during the day. This course of events allows you to step out of your comfort zone and habits to more easily assimilate these energies. Know that this change in sleeping habits will begin to dissipate as the energies settle into your physical body."

ଚ 📖 ଓ

Stay Clear

"Stay clear in your thinking. There has never been, nor shall there ever be, a separation of the One. You may appear to exist in physical form but this is merely an illusion of your own making. This illusion will dissipate in time as all come together to relish in the energies that now bombard your planet. The energies of Oneness and Light shall never again leave your realm of existence, no matter what the small mind of one may choose to experience. It is all good. It is all God. You are that of which it is.

"We are the Keeper of One here to rectify all ill-thought."

෨ 📖 ෫

The Galactic Federation Speaks

"You will trigger the truth that is deep inside you as these waves of consciousness expand your earth. The masses lie yet within the bounds of forgetfulness. But all those now ready step forth to awaken their thoughts of Wholeness, of Peace, of Love.

"As these days of massive change burst forth into the glory of awakening for many, let all sleeping dogs lie. In other words, do not seek out the illusions of past but prepare to go forth into the unknown, a place of greater living, greater BEing for all.

"We stand before you now ready to assist as desired. You have only to ask for our assistance to get it. The bands of consciousness on your earth are now ripe to burst into the glory of *All That Is*.

"Those ready to lead shall do so. Those ready to expand consciousness shall do so. And those yet unwilling to awaken to the truth of their BEing, as astute souls, shall remain asleep to awaken others. Bear no ill will upon any form as each has its own task to complete. Those with finished tasks shall move further, if only in mind, along the path of consciousness. This means, those finishing the task of their soul shall expand that soul's awareness, even as the physical form remains unaware of the greatness within.

"We are the Galactic Federation, as many refer to us, but only an illusion in your world. We come forth to assist those ready to believe in another aspect of Self, waiting for recognition. For those aware of the true illusion of fleeting forms, all shall carry on in perfect order as things on your earth unfold."

ജ 📖 ശ

The Host of One

"Things will be moving more quickly towards the end of your year 2014. Have faith in the morphing process as all go through this change at their own pace. You and many others shall bear the Light of Oneness more fully in coming days. Do not be concerned with those who appear distanced for they, in their own time, shall bear this Light of Oneness most fully in time.

"Take care to nurture your body as these changes take place. Allow enough time for rest, proper food and drink and be sure to relish in this Light to keep it glowing. As you move through this process your earth also changes with fervor. You are both becoming more in tune with other planets and multi-verses beyond your own solar system.

"Stay clear in your intentions and keep only enough to forge ahead in this New World of abundance for all humanity. This means, share any excess you may have with those who have nothing. Be aware of the great differences among those with more than they need and see that this unnecessary state of being only holds one back from knowing the truth of commitment to True Self. Your faith will carry you through these times as all things come into balance. Faith in Source, to provide all needs, is necessary at this time. Seek nothing outside your Self of One for all is illusion. This becomes increasingly clear to those not yet aware of other realms of being.

"We leave you with this thought: As your earth changes, be aware of body changes as well. Care for the Host of One putting all else aside and this shall carry you through to the New World of Peace, Abundance, Wonder, Wholeness and Joy.

"We are the Galactic Federation of Light here to help our brothers and sisters to fullness of BEing."

℘ 📖 ℘

True Legacy

"In time, disregarding the True Self leads to gross inadequacies. These appear as dis-ease within the physical frame. As time increases on your earth, more people will reveal this dis-ease. This is how one shall determine the nature of their progress, or lack thereof, toward True BEing.

"You are coming to a point in your own process, those of you who chose to morph physicality, where all will be known, before it occurs. Let not these times lead you to despair. For all is in Divine Order as earth moves more quickly toward its final thrust of glory to become more in tune with other planets.

"Seek not outside yourselves for the World Soul lies within waiting for recognition. This is but part of your true legacy, to be fully aware."

଼ 📖 ଓ

Use Your Imagination

"You will be traveling to those higher dimensions soon. All in your world changes as the physical body changes to be more in tune with the higher aspects of Reality.

"Your world is but a small part of the BEingness of *All That Is*. It is not a part of the Wholeness but you have chosen to play, as souls, in this physical reality. Now as your earth dimensions change, to be more in tune with Reality, so too must your body, to move with Mother Earth.

"These changes in physicality make it easier to travel out of body to other dimensions of time and space. Prepare for this event by going within, by using your mind to secure the vastness of time and space. Your imagination will serve as the first vehicle to move beyond form. Use this tool at your leisure and imagine the worlds you wish to visit. It makes no difference as to where the imagination goes for your essence knows the True Reality of BEing and shall lead you there in time."

৪০ 📖 ೞ

Ways of Being

"Higher, simpler ways of being are on the cusp of your awakening. These ways are made possible through the changes you now undergo, as physical frames morphing to a new structure. As these changes within you take place, do not be alarmed, for all is quite well. We are on the cusp of building a new paradigm, where all are as One encased in a frame of unheard of dimensions.

"Your world is now gone but soon to be replaced with one of a higher vibrational frequency, more in tune with other planets. All those upon earth now bear these gross changes or leave. There is no other choice for humanity now. As those willing to go forth and bear these changes, into new forms, increases, those not yet aware of the monumental move remain unaware of the occurrence. Keep in mind that few chose this path. But all will eventually sense and undergo the changes those ready to do so now face.

"Your world is but a measure of distance from creating newer realities of abundance, created by faith and trust in *All That Is*. Let not the fleeting signs of distain and limitation affect your vibration. For this time in your history now comes to an end. Speak not of the separation seen so clearly in mass media but know each soul is indeed your counterpart, ready to assimilate back to Wholeness and Truth. For you are That of which It is.

"We thank you for your efforts, knowing that for a human in physicality it is not an easy task. The time has come. Your days upon this earth are numbered in ways of old turning to ways of greater truths. All now hold the Light within to some extent. But some hold much more of that essence of Oneness to lead the way for those uncertain of their roots."

ɞ 📖 ɞ

You Are Not Alone

"Understand, no one goes through this process alone. We stand before you, leading the way to the glory of Self. As these days quickly unfold in your world, be prepared to go further than ever before along the path of freedom. All stand in readiness (from other realms) to assist as needed.

"Let not the small mind of one hold you back for all is coming to fruition quickly. We come together in a new frequency to assist those ready to move forward. In coming days, all will unfold, for some in chaos, for others in sheer delight. Knowing your place in the grand scheme of things will enable a more fluid movement toward the BEingness of *All That Is*.

"Trust in the process to carry you through to the Divine Oneness of which you seek. Enable others along this path by freely sharing your news of Wholeness, Peace, and Love. For those unable or unwilling to move forward along this path, the BEingness of One remains, if ever so silently within.

"Prepare to become more than ever before as these monumental changes take place on your earth. Many are now ready to step forward, within your own ranks, to assist with the changes being made. Your grand gesture, to secure the Oneness of Life within, shall become increasingly clear, as all move through this time of great change.

"Recall, there is no duality in the Oneness of fluid Life. This shall remain so as you seem to move through darkness to reach greater aspects of Light."

ଈୄ 📖 ଈୄ

~ Part Two ~
Author's Experiences

3-D is Over

This waking message reminds me that we live in various parallel dimensions. I truly believe what we accomplish in this realm affects other realms.

"The time is here for all to hear, to speak the Truth of One. Your time in the 3-D world is now over with this new wave of Love and Light from outer realms. You are now entering the Golden Age of Gaia more fully."

Sleep came again. I woke to recall a dream of being with Ruth and Daniel as everyone prepared for a disaster. We looked out a large picture window (from a Florida house lived in thirty-one years ago) to see a large, black cloud in the distance to our right (over the ocean). But it then seemed to disappear. Everyone was preparing stupid, little places to hunker down in. I saw water levels rising and pointed them out to Daniel who said there was an unreported earthquake near Cuba. We had to look for eight-year-old Rebecca who appeared to have been sleeping across the street with a boy named Jack. (Her ex-fiancé's name was Jack.) I told the children to now forget that stuff for we needed to get with family to do things to stay alive.

Another message came upon waking after falling back asleep.

"Feed only those energies you wish to exist. The path is steady and true for you now.

Use it wisely to make better decisions. Know that you, as all lightworkers, starseeds, and wayshowers, are watched over carefully. Prepare to meet circumstances unheard of, as to date, by remaining centered within your Self of One.

"All things on your earth now change rapidly. Know that, as you travel this new path, guides will be there to help you along the way. All things in time must now repeat to be cleared and cleansed forevermore. This means you shall be faced with situations where it is up to you to make better decisions than in the past.

"Know that all upon your earth will not withstand the great changes now occurring. But you, as a worker of Light, are to be there for those willing to forego new ways of living and being. Stay clear in your intention to help those along the path of One by remaining within your own world of grace and ease. Know that not all have this advantage to be a clear channel of Love and Light.

"We bid you adieu for now. We are your brothers and sisters in Light, parts of you long forgotten by Soul but nevertheless existing on other realms of this reality."

✡

A Good Friday Personal Message

Energies remain intense but walks on the beach help me to merge with the heartbeat of Mother Earth. A Good Friday personal message comes after asking for one.

"Each has their own role to play. The role you now play softens the hearts of those initiates willing to move forward with their evolution. We are, in essence, a part of the Whole of *All That Is*, finding our way, slowly for some, back to the grandness and greatness of Self. This Self is a part of each human being and ready to express on greater levels. You give the initiates the opportunity to do this with your words and deeds. Your thoughts must be kept wholly on the work of Oneness. Do not stray into the field of duality but remain steadfast in your efforts to help others recognize their True Self.

"Each human being is now ready to move forward, so to speak. Some will move forward out of the physical leaving earth, some will remain to help others, and others will move through the maze lost in the sea of forgetfulness. Be not concerned as these necessary circumstances take place but know all is within the realm of Oneness, not yet expressed fully by those playing the game.

"We bid you adieu. We are a part of you."

✡

A Necessary Course

It's been a long time since I wrote in my journal due to various reasons, ranging from disinterest to another tooth issue. Yet, today on January 1, 2014, the new apartment's CD player begins to act erratically so I turn on the laptop to take the message, which comes very quickly.

"Verily I say onto you, do not be discouraged by the current state of events for all in your world quickly changes to an unrecognizable state for many beings of Light. This state of affairs shall not last for long, as previously reported, but is, as yet, a necessary course of events to get all to the state of awareness of Self. This Self, as many now know, was lost in the fray of remembering when humanity took on denser and denser forms.

"You shall, as many others, lead the way back to wholeness of Self as all return to a state of Wholeness from gross disarray. Purging old habits serves one best at this time as you move through this process. No one is left behind and yet all are One in Wholeness and Truth of *Reality*.

"You shall experience waves of gross earth disturbances, as before, but this shall be much different for much has changed in your atmosphere. We are watching from other states of awareness as many continue to try and manipulate the unknowing masses of those still unconsciousness to True BEing. You must be aware that each soul, although as you know is illusion, has its own purpose and meaning. Each soul has a task to complete as these times spurt forth. Do not be preoccupied with those yet asleep but remain focused on your task. Each shall know their task in their own time. Many shall complete it without knowing the meaning of action and awareness. Never relate to the chaos as it erupts but be clear on your own goal, whatever that may be. Stay clear in your own awareness of Truth and Light as we all move further from the illusion through chaos.

"Be it said today, on all levels great changes take place because of those awakened souls on earth. You are looked upon as gracious beings of Light and we are with you all the way.

"We are the souls of One."

✡

Archangel Michael Speaks

Of this, I am certain. I am a figment of *All That Is* here to experience, express and expand the richness of my so-called soul. And yet, all here is illusion! Yesterday was the third Angel News Network class on the "Laws of BEingness" and this morning the first message from Archangel Michael came though me.

"You are nurturing the grandness of Self, the greatness of Self, as you go through this process of Self awakening. Be ever mindful of the gifts you have to offer. They lie inside your very being and it is up to you to uncover and use them as these great waves of change take place upon your earth.

"Each figment of the Whole holds these gifts to uncover and display to the other figments of the Whole. Each figment now awakens to the grandness and greatness of Self as it awakens to its True Essence. You may now test the waters of Truth and True Beingness as these actions of Love and Light pour forth.

"I am Archangel Michael here to serve you as you serve your Self."

✡

As I Please

After napping, a message comes when I ask a question as to what can I bring down to this life from other lives of greater consciousness.

"You are bringing forth through these downloads. Stay steady, the course."

Energies seem intense, knocking me out to sleep more, with much better sleep at night and rest periods, these past few days. At one point, after blowing my nose, I got extremely dizzy and had to carefully move to the sectional two feet away, else I'd fall down. The room was spinning and it was as if my ears were blocked and ringing as usual. Sleeping hours remain erratic but I do not concern myself for I am alone and can do as I please!

✡

Building the Lightbody

Dawn breaks after a long night of rest in mid-March 2014, rising to drink water and eliminate it about every two hours, after asking to incorporate the Lightbody with ease and grace to the fullest degree. A channeled message begins.

"As the Lightbody forms, you will begin to feel a tingling. This can often feel as if you have the flu. Each nerve of your body is firing in a different manner to incorporate more of the Light that you truly are. You may feel this as pinpricks or gross feelings of unease within body cells. Drink plenty of water and be sure to rest as needed to withstand this process more smoothly.

"This is a process never before experienced on your earth and you must take it slowly to incorporate all aspects successfully without undue effects. The body is not accustomed to these DNA changes and many people feel as if they are sick. Stay within your own system of belief and do not venture into the territory of old school thought. For each unnatural substance incorporated into the physical frame will delay the process. You must trust in your own ability to withstand and undergo these changes without depending on others to carry you through.

"The process of returning to Light can be smooth for those with full trust. Be aware of those that lead others to beliefs that delay or mar the process by taking certain substances.

You do not require or need any unnatural substance to withstand this process. Go with the body's natural flow of cohesion (unity, organization, pulling together)."

There really is no name for this energy but I chose to name it Amanda.

✡

Choices and Reaction

It's been an interesting time as humanity faces many old wounds to offer new growth opportunities. The third of April found me at a new car repair shop for a second estimate on what could have been two oil leaks, with a possibility of nearly $2K in costs. The mechanic told me one looked more serious and offered a repair estimate of $100 less than the first shop. I made the appointment for the following day since it involved oil leaking onto the distributor (the part that literally runs the entire car).

Friday morning found me up earlier than usual, after a somewhat restless night full of energies, but not tired at all. Happy two hours later, after charging nearly $700 to my credit card and learning there was no second leak, I stopped to get mail at the Post Office.
"Service engine soon" a warning light noted as the car started.
Of course, I drove right back to the mechanic, knowing fully there was good reason and I was to remain heart-centered. The mechanic told me sometimes it takes a bit of time for the car's computer to "kick-in."
"Start it up about twenty times and put some miles on it," he said with a knowledgeable smile, "and bring it back if the light stays on."
Each day I woke near dawn again and decided to keep it that way for summer is coming. It's always good to rise early to get things done before afternoon heat sets in. Six days later, I knew the light would remain on for

this was an opportunity for me to clear old wounds. It was time to fully let go of victim mentality. I sent runners and angels before me, drove to the shop, and arrived right after it opened.

The mechanic popped his head up out of the garage as I arrived. His face broke out into a slight smile.

"Light's still on," he noted. "I've got another new distributor right here. I thought the first one might have been bad and ordered it in case you returned. It will take less than an hour to replace."

Unfortunately, the garage filled with cars from the previous day so I needed to return the next morning. Again, I looked at it as another opportunity to cement new waking hours and remain heart-centered.

That evening I participated in the local Course of Miracles class and, of course, the opportunity rose to share my car repair story along with other events.

I was full of love upon arriving at the car repair shop the next morning. Someone else was already there but the mechanic began my repair as promised. The shop owner and several customers arrived during the next hour, all before the mechanic appeared with a look of utter dismay.

"I took your car for a test drive," he said with authority, "but it just plain stalled out down the street. I called my tow-truck guy and he's going to tow it back here. It must be another bad distributor. At least it happened to me and not you!"

71

"Ah," I thought smiling, "happy ego is looking for a reaction."

The mechanic told me someone would drive me home and he'd take care of the car.

At one point, minutes later, the shop's owner addressed me, full of empathy.

"I'm sorry this happened. I sent both my mechanics down the street, with the first distributor, to get your car back here. I can drive you home if you like while we take care of your car."

He sounded so sincere. I decided to stay and watch things unfold.

"It's not your fault," I told the now very upset, red-faced, overweight man as he trudged back to his office to cough.

The mechanic appeared in what seemed like less than ten minutes later.

"I can drive you home if you want but another new distributor should be here in ten minutes and I'll get you out of here in twenty."

I decided to stay and wait knowing there was a reason. My treasured friend Phillip answered my phone call to verify that yes; this was another opportunity to release and heal negative emotion, to remain heart-centered.

Coughing sounds erupted from the office as I felt the owner's dismay minutes later. He moved toward me to apologize again, such a sweet man and yet afraid of marring his shop's good reputation. I could tell he dealt with many egos that always looked for someone else to blame. He always took things personally and allowed his physical health to suffer because of it.

Yes, another opportunity to do God's work presented itself as I replied!

True to his word, the mechanic brought my car to the door after twenty minutes. I drove home happy to know I'd made a difference in someone's life.

"Service engine soon," the warning light noted when I drove to the Farmer's Market the next day.

Obviously, there was more to experience.

Dawn broke on Monday morning as a message flowed.

"It isn't about the choices you make but the reaction you have of the experiences you chose. Reactions in and of themselves speak of a world of duality. To move ahead into the land of freedom one must go with the flow, knowing all experience is a part of the experience chosen by soul to bring one back to full alignment. Every chance encounter, every planned meeting is with ones self, for all are One in an unerring stream of Love, waiting for recognition.

"Take not your experience as that of harmful, but know all is in Divine Order as you move forward on the illusory scale of evolution with the recognition that you meet only your self with each seeming separate person you encounter."

I soon send runners and angels before me, envisioning a free oil change somewhere down the line. After pulling into the shop's drive, the determined mechanic notes he must now fully test the car with a machine to find a short. He might need to buy a part. Again, it will not cost me a thing. The process will take three hours but someone will drive me home so I won't have to wait in the non-air-conditioned building. And, he adds, I might just get a free oil change for all my time and trouble.

"This is a blessing," I think.

Yes, there's good reason for all of this to happen and tomorrow it will unfold.

Sleeping is easier and I wake shortly after five o'clock in the morning. It seems impossible to sleep again so I rise for breakfast. Yet, an hour after eating, returning to bed sounds good for I'm drowsy and it's nearly sixty minutes before I need to dress and drive to the car repair shop. Thirty minutes later I rise, envisioning a simple repair, where I will not be shuttled home or wait long. I don't know how it will unfold but know that all is well.

Just as envisioned, the car saga ends. It turns out to be a defective part within the new distributors, which the mechanic replaces without cost. By now he's tripled the time spent on my car, and fine-tuned it, and I've remained heart-centered throughout the process.

"I won't see you again for another 2,000 miles, when you get the oil changed," he announces with a grin.

"Everything is an opportunity," I tell the shop owner before leaving. "We just need to figure out what the opportunity is."

I don't share that for me it was to choose Love instead of the age-worn habit of fear.

All is well as we increase the vibrational field of earth after a lunar eclipse, in the midst of a full moon, and prior to a solar eclipse and Grand Cardinal Cross.

"Service engine soon" the warning light notes once again upon starting the car.

✡

Discern Thy Truths

Once again, the CD player malfunctions in my new sanctuary by the sea. Of course, I stop to document the message.

"Listen to thy body to discern thy truths. Each body occurrence, whether it be of illness or emotional dis-ease arises from emotional and mental anguish housed within the mass consciousness, including any housed within the ethers of your own experience throughout this experiment of separation from Source. Pay attention to these occurrences and know that we, the Consciousness of *All That Is*, are here to help alleviate the false pressures you have placed upon your small self of one. Let all emotional distress expend itself as you feel those feelings, claim them as part of the experience, and move on to the Wholeness and Truth of other games within your illusion.

"We are here to help those ready to move forward and look ahead to working with you at your leisure. Call upon us as desired to move forward into the maze of life on earth.

"We are the Consciousness of One."

✡

Do Things Differently

Tooth infection and pain, despite a root canal and crown prompts me to ask for clarification as to why it is occurring.

"Wholeness is greatness and greatness is *All That Is*. As you move further into this greatness, you must let go of old ways of being. These habits have kept humanity in the throes of limitation for far too long.

"It is time to do things differently, to count upon your own I AM Presence to lead the way to greatness. You must listen to this Voice of Reason above all else as your days turn quickly into the darkness of night in all aspects. These days will not last long but you shall experience them as lost aspects of Self, now coming forward to be recognized as the Wholeness of Self.

"These aspects were left behind many lives ago to deviate in bodily pleasures and experience aspects not felt before in human form. The time to fully incorporate these aspects is here. You and others will feel these changes as painful experiences, which lead one to the trueness of Self. For all is indeed ready to burst forth into greater aspects of Self in the Now.

"Be ye not afraid as these changes occur but know you are one of many who now lead the masses toward great change. This change, again, is about doing things differently. Make sure you do all things differently than before to clear old aspects of being. Recognize each choice as a means to freedom of Self expression, experience, and greatness of Self."

As the pain intensifies, I recognize any pain as something that held me back, that limited me. Now I recognize it as something that helps to spur this form toward greater living by foregoing the usual route of relief. It is time to accept pain as a part of the experience, but not let it limit our BEing. We must all allow experiences of this type to teach us that we can rise above the limitation we set upon ourselves so long ago.

It is time to take back our power and recognize that we are Gods of Matter with the ability to free ourselves. We need believe in the old ways no longer for now is the time to live in the New World of freedom in all things.

"I am the I AM Presence, on the New Earth in the New World, and I am ever so grateful."

"These words will assist you in walking through the portal of time and space with ease and grace as your earth continues to evolve at rapid rates."

✡

Downloads Abound

During a very restless night, in April 2014 waking with extreme thirst, drinking water, eliminating it, and returning to sleep, I wake near five o'clock in the morning upon hearing "Sit up to receive."

"It's to get another download," I think, recalling an earlier one. But a message begins.

"You are receiving a great amount of information. Care for the physical host with utmost attention. This process will not last long but will occur in steady bouts throughout the year 2014. You must know that all things on your earth change quickly now as these downloads occur. You are not the only one receiving these downloads of Love and Grace from higher realms.

"Prepare to care for your physical host in new ways by paying attention to your energy field. Avoid areas of lower vibrating fields and beware of those who strive to lower humanity's vibration. These instances will lessen in time on your earth as people learn to avoid that which they no longer wish to experience again. All lie in readiness to help those of humanity who wish to progress on the scale of evolution. But for those unaware of the changing field of ever-present change, the circumstances around them will increase to an uproar of undue harm. Pay no heed to this occurrence for all is not lost but merely gained on a different scale of evolution.

"That is all for now my loved one. Let all know these changes are a necessary occurrence to morph your consciousness to the necessary pace to keep up with earth. All is well in the only realm of One that never changes and that is your True State of awareness.

"We are the Keeper of One here to assist those ready to move forward."

We are in the midst of more earth changes, on the cusp of two eclipses with a full moon and Grand Cardinal Cross (aligning of four planets and the moon) between them. Energies continue to increase as many of us reinvent ourselves. Selected signs of a morphing form now include:

- Light in peripheral vision.

- Extreme thirst upon rising during the night.

- A strong sense of receiving downloads of information, numbers, and related data.

- A desire to care for your body by changing lifestyle habits.

- Increased body heat originating from the chest.

- Increased body vibration and ear ringing.

- Occasional nausea, intestinal discomfort, ascension diarrhea or headache.

- Increased desire to help others.

✡

Due Diligence

A message from higher realms of belief barrels through the grid as I wake near dawn, consider walking on the beach and reject the idea for tomorrow my sister joins me in the ritual.

"As you motor through these pathways of change, keep in mind the physical body is a Host of One. This does not preclude you from being human but does allow you to take steps to improve your lot in life and remain within the ethers of your reality as well. This means you must always be aware of the need to support yourself, and your process, in the best possible way through due diligence. Due Diligence is taking action, when needed, to keep the Host of One purely in a state of True Consciousness, by steering clear of any outside influence.

"The times before you now are a mixture of ecstasy and agony for many in your world. You must be ready and able to help those parts of yourself improve their lot in life as well by listening and advising as requested. This process is a necessary one to keep all apart from the dire consequences of separation. For recall, you are part of one another, reaching out to congeal back to Oneness in all aspects.

"We are the Keeper of One, ever ready to assist. Namaste."

✡

Express Your Self Fully

As light glows in my peripheral vision at dusk, I choose to channel. A question forms. What is in the best interests of all selves to concentrate on at this time?

"The One of *All That Is* awaits your decision to express fully in the moment of Now, holding nothing back, being ever aware that what you think manifests into full BEingness of Self in all aspects. Your task on this plane, at this time, is to fully express the small self of one and to exist on greater levels than ever before. Pay attention to old habits keeping you locked into the fray of past efforts. Know that each thought, each decision, each action creates another thought, word, deed that expresses on this and other levels of awareness.

"Know that you alone hold the key to full BEing and must express that now as earth readies herself to yet again expand into the Light of One. Your world changes quickly as all watch from other realms of your existence. Let all things move forward in a pace rather slowly for some and rather quickly for others. It is not up to any one soul to change the world but to change their thought system back to the purity of Oneness from whence it came.

"We bid you good day knowing we are aspects of your self, waiting on other realms to incorporate with you more fully. Namaste."

✡

Golden Light Downloads

A message fills my head upon waking at dawn.

"Remember to download the golden Light into your crown each day to assimilate these higher frequencies more easily. As these changes take place on your earth, you and many others lead the way to greatness of BEing, living in the Light of One, with Truth and Honesty, sharing the Love of One with all humanity, and reaping the rewards thereof"

✡

Ground Crew Message

"Continue to rid yourself of those possessions that reek of duality. Remember the Oneness of all life and be careful with your thoughts. You alone are responsible for your world. If you are unhappy with things in your world, it is up to you to change your thought process, to focus on the Oneness of Life, to be the spirit that you truly are for it is only in this process of becoming that one may rid themselves of the perils of duality while still in human form.

"Do not pay heed to those that seem outside you but realize all is illusion of the small mind of one ever striving to keep you in the duality of limitation. You are not a single entity, as it seems, but much more than imagined. These next fourteen days are crucial to humanity's awakening. Many doorways now open to allow those with eyes to see. You must open these doorways to your heart and mind to avoid the mass illusion that now thickens around this world.

"All lie in readiness to help those ready to walk through the doorways of Light and Love. Seek help from your brothers and sisters of Light for ways to pass through these doorways effortlessly as they have. Your journey now changes to one of abundance without limit as you enter these times. But for those remaining beyond the veil of illusion it remains a quite different story, a much different reality.

"Seek only to change your own illusion for others around you have not chosen to walk through the doorways of Light and yet, each has its own role to awaken the mass consciousness yet asleep. Know that you hold the key to your own liberty. Free your mind of gross misunderstanding and walk through the doorways of Light to the Spring of Awareness.

"I am the Keeper of One here to help those ready to awaken to True BEing.

"Namaste."

Upon transcribing this message in March 2014, I get the distinct impression that there will always be doorways opening for those upon earth. It is just a matter of when each person becomes aware of the ascension process and chooses to enter those states of increased awareness. To walk through the doorways of Oneness:

- Rid yourself of all possessions and memories of separation (any strong ties that do not serve your highest good). Examine each possession, relationship, and memory for reactions keeping you in ego awareness (this includes special love relationships keeping you in co-dependant lifestyles).

- Practice conscious thinking by feeding only those thoughts you wish to exist in your New World.

- Assess lifestyle to omit practices that do not nurture the human form (such as smoking, alcohol, excessive food intake, leisure time activities, etc.).

- Begin a practice of silently blessing others with Love and Light. Visualize them as parts of yourself waiting to be loved and recognized as the Light of One.

- Remain steadfast in your desire to know only the positive aspects of BEing.

- Remember a smile or kind word is always appreciated.

- Nourish the body and soul with healthy food and water, proper sleep, and periods of listening (meditation) to get guidance needed to make the transition to Light.

- Avoid groups of unawakened souls engaged in feeding energies that are not life affirming.

- Take time to go out into nature or tend your own garden of inside plants.

Remember, you alone hold the key to your awakening. As these times unfold, earth changes will continue to make it tedious for those still lost in the illusion of mass consciousness. Remain within your own field of reality and hone that field continuously by taking in golden Light from the top of your head and sending it through your feet, around your physical frame, and back through the head. This will help you to remain encased within the Light that you are rather than take in the energies of those around you.

✡

Honing the Lightbody

Naps have been less frequent but sleeping hours erratic, especially after working on a video until 3:30 am on Saturday. Now I can again begin to wake earlier with the goal of walking on the beach near dawn. But today, I could not function properly without a nap and drifted off two hours after eating a late breakfast. It's now nearly 7:30 PM and I am again feeling tired and so I ask, "Why?"

"Dense energies portray thoughts of mass consciousness. You, as many others, are prone to pick up these energies making you more tired than usual. Your situation is unique in that it is also honing the lightbody in a new way, more pronounced than many, yet slower than others. You must be aware of not only your thoughts but your propensity to remain in the drama of old energies, making it more difficult to incorporate these energies of Light within the physical frame.

"Know we are with you and shall continue to guide and watch over you. Yes, sleep as necessary but know this too shall pass. We are aware that it has been years for you, years of feeling tired after eating, but again, the adrenals are getting a workout from these changes, just continue your new regimen of herbs and salts and know it will help with the process of returning to the level of light you desire.

"We are the White-Winged Consciousness of Nine ready to assist as all move forward, so to speak, to Light."

✡

Humanity's True Source of Power

Taking the time to channel always seems to be last on my list of things to do. So today, after walking on the beach, I follow though with my new intention to set aside time to channel higher realms within my illusion. This is the result at dusk.

"Through the ethers of space we come to greet you on this day. We are the Galactic Federation of Light, your brothers and sisters on yet another realm of illusion.

"Be clear in your intentions as all things old fall away. Do not replace these systems with old habits but design and work though new systems more in tune with the Light of Love that you are. All things on your realm now quickly fall away to be replaced by greater systems, some yet to be discovered. But be clear in your intentions to use these systems in new ways, no longer relinquishing your God-given power but knowing you are a part of that Power. There is not, nor has there ever been, a need to relinquish your Power to any source beyond your Self. Humanity holds the Power of One within. It is the true heritage of humanity to find and use as desired.

"We leave you with this thought. Determine your true Source of Power and use this source to design a life free of all limitations, for it is only in your small self of one that limitation exists."

Our true Source of Power is our ability to use free will wisely, to change old habits and ways of living, to return to a simpler way of life. Of, this I am most certain.

✡

Incorporating Light

After visiting the acupuncturist for a treatment and herbs, tiredness comes again the next day upon eating breakfast. Of course, usual ego dialogue tries to convince me there's something seriously wrong. I'm very grateful for the message that flows easily from head to hands.

"It's a process, the process of returning to Light. As you move through this process, know you are one of many choosing to do so. You will feel tired at times as the body readjusts to waking moments after sleep, traveling in other dimensions of your reality to gather those parts of you together to hold more Light. These occurrences are often felt more easily after eating as the body adjusts its processes (from sleeping to waking) to run smoothly. Your body is not accustomed to working on higher realms, taking in Light, which requires no food or drink. As you move through this process, the body must adjust to both worlds while still in physical form.

"Be kind to yourself. Rest as needed and be sure to incorporate the streams of Light that come each morning upon waking. These streams are helping you to adjust to physical life while still in human form. Be sure to drink plenty of water and eat lighter foods of natural substances, fruits, vegetables, easily digested proteins, such as nuts and seeds to help the process along.

"We bid you adieu for now knowing all is as it should be as you, one of many, incorporate the Light more fully.

"We are the White-Winged Consciousness of Nine."

✡

Invisible Matrix of Life

Once again, it seems that after eating breakfast extreme tiredness soon causes me to sleep for sixty to ninety minutes. I always wake to recall being on other realms of illusion, often teaching or serving others. Today I ask for words of wisdom on how to motor through this matrix with ease, grace, and abundant energy. The following words flow through me easily.

"Each soul has its own journey in this invisible matrix of life. While you wait in heavy silence, or noise depending upon your focus, it is always best to keep in mind that Spirit is ever near. Your world exists solely within your small self of one. This is not to negate your physical form (to make it less than valuable), but to note that this physical form is always striving to keep ego alive and well. One must recall that ego is yet another ploy in the game of separation.

"To motor through this matrix of what you refer to as life, remember all you see is a valuable part of you. It makes no difference as to the role played for all roles lead to the same path of Oneness and Light. Each moves along this path at their soul's own speed. Take nothing for granted as you motor along the path of Oneness but always recall you are that of which *It* is, already perfect, whole and complete. It is only in the recognition, the gross feeling, of this nature that you shall recognize this truth in its fullness.

"We are the Galactic Federation of Light, in the form of many beings together enhancing the journey of those who ask for our assistance."

✡

Keeper of One Speaks

I wake near dawn to hear words repeating in my brain. Usually this occurs each morning but I often fall back asleep. Obviously, one key to channeling other realms is to get a proper night's sleep! Today I ask who wishes to interact with me and hear it is the Keeper of One. The following message flows slowly as I repeat it into a bedside tape recorder.

"Allow me to allow you to relish in the Oneness. This Oneness of which I speak surrounds you on a daily basis. It is the Oneness of all life, all beings, every environment of space and time. Allow yourself to relish in this Oneness as things go awry, as you would say. This Oneness is the true nature of all humanity, of all life, of all things in and out of time and space.

"The days before you now are fraught with the measures of undue, what you would refer to as, harm. These measures shall last but for a very short time before all quickly changes to become closer to the Oneness in which all within the Reality of One live. Your time on earth is beginning to change drastically. As these days before you go smoothly and effortlessly towards the BEingness of Oneness, let all things fall into place effortlessly. Know that you are the keeper of your own Oneness. There is none other but you to relish in this Oneness of Love, of Light, of unconditional living within the realms of Oneness.

"Pay no heed to what goes on around you, unless of course it detrimentally affects your own very survival, your own very being. And yet, as this occurs, one must always remain within the heart. Take the practical steps you feel you need to survive in your world but know that all is truly illusion of your own making. As a soul, you have chose a lovely and varied game of lessons, of experiences, of karmic relationships, of karmic deeds to do and undo, and yet as you move through these days know that all is illusion. Your thoughts make this illusion. Your dreams help you to relish in the Oneness.

"Be clear in your thinking for every thought is an electrical charge that manifests on some level of reality, your reality. Every thought may be positive, relishing in the Oneness of all life, or negative, wallowing in the separation of fear. Choose love and stay in your heart space to forgo what many now succumb to. Choose love and relish in the Oneness for these days shall not last long but shall affect all on earth. Know this and remain within your heart feeling that Oneness of all life and knowing each condition, each circumstance, each person you interact with reveals a part of your own consciousness. Keep thoughts within the realms of Oneness, of Love, of Light and know that all is ultimately very, very well.

"I am the Keeper of One and I bid you good day."

Today, I am knowing all is in perfect and Divine Order as I continue in this gaseous state knowing this body morphs, feeling these aches and pains. And yet according to other sources, seeming to be apart from me on Facebook, they are the very things experienced by others. In fact, I am quite lucky for many others report many more signs of morphing, and serious ones at that. I am grateful for all the wonderful things that continue to come into my life and I know all is in Divine Order. It can be no other way!

✡

Love and Light Downloads

Another night of waking every two hours unfolds but this, for me, is a usual state and much preferred to nights of waking every few minutes instead. I seem to rest easier these past two nights even though the trusty satellite Internet booster blinks orange several times, letting me know we are indeed experiencing massive inflows of energy. For those of us thinking the energies are dissipating, it's time to think again, for now it's becoming increasingly clear that they are not. We are just handling them better than ever before, or not!

A message begins shortly after eight o'clock in the morning after I wake for the sixth time.

"There will be more downloads of Love and Light onto your planet as these energies continue to change. Your world is now on a massive movement toward the BEingness of *All That Is*. It will be, as you say, a Wild Ride. Prepare yourself by moving within. Do not pay mind to the circumstances around you but know all is in Divine Order as Mother Earth returns to her pristine state. This will, unfortunately, take many years. But recall, in your true state of BEing it is but a blink of an eye.

"Know that you are being carefully watched over as all your earth systems change to incorporate this massive flow of Love and Light. It is not in your, or anyone's, best interest to participate in the ploys of

98

separation. Therefore, be ever ready to receive these downloads knowing all are ultimately One BEing, untouched and unseparated. So be it now and forevermore as all coalesce back to the Perfection of what many refer to as God.

"Take this time to rest as these energies allow and know all is well in your true state of Nirvana.

"We are the Keeper of One here to help all adjust to a new way of BEing in human form."

✡

Love is the Propeller

Sleep is impossible. So I rise, filled with a great sense that something is amiss on earth. I must forgo the usual morning rituals to post inspiring messages and tools to increase the body's vibration on Facebook.

Words flow after making breakfast an hour later. They seem as if coming from the usual me, but flow more easily than usual.

"Even for those fully aware that this is an illusion, there's still a strong sense of love and duty to those parts of us still lost within the dream. Hence, it seems necessary to help each soul as much as possible to set their, and our, mind/body at ease that all is well, that we are a part of one another, never separated, not by space nor time, nor circumstances. And so I move forward into this new life of Rev. SAM knowing full well all things may change. And yet, it's all good!"

Extreme tiredness plagues me during the day (multiple solar flares erupt the day before Easter 2014). I take two short naps, remembering multi-dimensional interactions upon waking. A walk on the beach helps to ground before working on a new section of the website. "So many people still seem to sleep within the dream," I think, working and recalling multiple families interacting with technology on the beach.

Another message comes at twilight.

"As you take this next step in your evolution be aware that others do not take the same steps as you and others. The times on your earth are building to a crescendo of fury for those lost in the maze of forgetfulness. Do not let this deter you from your task as lightworkers and wayshowers. Do not allow yourselves to be turned from your own work of bearing the Light of One. You must maintain your vibration at all costs. This may mean stepping back from family situations you may have helped with in the past. Recall, each soul chose their journey before birth. It is not up to you to change any circumstance or situation by your presence, nor advice. It may be best for all to step away and let things unfold in a timely manner.

"We are the Keeper of One here to assist those requesting our help. You need only ask to receive."

✡

New Ways of BEing

This message came from a different energy than what I am accustomed to channeling. It was a bit harder to incorporate as body heat increased and eyesight diminished. It's rhythm seemed more mental than those channeled previously. As you begin to tap into the higher realms of Reality be prepared for different rhythms. And always go with those that resonate with you.

"Taken into first place are the tiny specks of Light that we all are originally. The days upon you now change with increasing fervor to change old ways. New ways of BEing break through the ethers of space as these changes occur more rapidly. Your place in the grand scheme of things is to assure that these changes are natural and part of the process of becoming that of which you really are. This state of BEing was left many, many eons ago to deviate into the earthly pleasures many now succumb to.

"All things on your earth are not circumspect, in that many things are hidden from those unaware of gross manipulation. This change of BEing has become more rapid over the eons of time that humanity left knowledge of Self to play new games of pleasure and power. These times are coming to an end quickly as what you refer to as Higher Beings assist. Those ready to acknowledge their True Self now move forward at a rapid pace, helping all to recognize the Truth of BEing, while the manipulators continue their game. There is no real Truth on your earth. This will become increasingly evident to those not able to see through the false maze of being in earthly form.

"Take care in the days ahead and know you are but one of many who now move into place to secure your rightful place. These days will not last long but they will be tiresome at best.

"I am a being who left your earth long ago after seeding the planet. This means I am a part of you who helped to put this earth into form. The closest I have to a name is Amanda but in those times, we did not have names to identify ourselves. You shall be okay. Don't worry about your future. It is already taken care of. Just go with the flow and stay in your heart."

✡

One with *All That Is*

Still sensing an unseen struggle within the world, I rise at dawn to hear children searching for Easter eggs next door. Thoughts of the future and pending expenses rise minutes before a message flows through the ever-thinning veil of forgetfulness.

"You are one with *All That Is*. There is no need to fear. As your earth changes many of you shall leave to play the game of physical life again, in another space and time. Some of you shall return to the fuller aspects of *All That Is* as part of the Whole. Many of you shall stay on your planet to forge ahead into the New World of Love and Light. It is your soul's chosen destiny, for this life, to help others through the new energies and to cement a new way of BEing, a way of greater living in all aspects.

"Do not fear as these times unfold for each soul is housed within an undeniable system of Wholeness and Truth. It may not be apparent on your earth at this time but Truth never changes. It just is, perfect, Whole and complete. You are, and always have been, a part of this Truth. Do not be swayed by what occurs for in essence you have never left the Wholeness and Love of *All That Is*."

But how does that help humanity get through these times when money or other necessities seem needed?

"Just know you are all included in that vast network many refer to as the God Network. Your needs will always be taken care of despite your beliefs in a system of greed and deceit that ruled your earth for so long. Be immersed in the Oneness of *All That Is* and know the God Network continues to provide for those in need. It may not offer what you are accustomed to but it will keep you out of the fear and deceit many lost in the dream now succumb to.

"You have all you need to carry out your soul's chosen journey. Know you are never alone for we, of the Light of Truth, are always with you."

✡

Open Your Mind

Sleep comes before midnight but I rise a few times before four o'clock in the morning and then am unable to sleep again. I finally turn on the laptop after five to get a message.

"The outer realms of possibility exist for all humanity. It is merely a means of asking that you shall receive. Seek and you shall find. Open your mind to greater possibilities, greater illusion (for all is illusion), greater ways of living and existing. It is only in one limited mind/body that you seem to relish in old habits of non-manifestation. Keep thoughts on the life you wish to live, envision it fully, and make sure you do nothing to betray that vision in your thoughts or deeds. For it is only in your mind that this vision exists and without the steady vision of desires nothing takes place. Do you understand this? Do you know that each thought creates a substance?

"The greater aspects of living are already yours to keep. All you need do is listen to the voice within and follow that unerring guidance. Prepare your host for moving forward on all levels of illusory being for that is where you are now. Get ready to relish in the Light of One more fully as these energies settle within your physical frame and know we are ever with you, guiding, supporting, and caring for your very soul of one."

✡

Personal Message

Sleeping is very erratic as geomagnetic activity heightens during the full moon and lunar eclipse. It's easier to sleep on April 16, 2014 and after about six hours, I wake shortly after five o'clock in the morning. A personal message begins.

"It is time to gather the initiates. This is your true task here to gather together all those ready to move forward on the scale of evolution. You shall do this with your new website as time on earth wears on to a fury of pain for many. Do not be concerned with this course of events for all is in order. Your task is of the utmost concern for those souls not yet ready to see their own power. The following of ages past will no longer be available for them to see but a new awakening to the grandness of Self, the greatness of Self, the glory of One, shall be revealed to all humankind as days progress to nights and nights to days.

"Just sense and feel. You are carefully guided and watched over. We are the Brotherhood of One ready to assist all toward the greatness of I AM."

✡

Reality Check

Inner guidance prompts me to begin storing information for a new website section. The words flow easily from head to typing fingers.

"What would you do if perfect strangers verified thoughts and intuition? What if you recognized that each person you meet, each person who interacts with you, nods or smiles as you pass, speaks, or otherwise engages you, is really a part of you, with a message to relate? Would you begin to recognize the path of ever-increasing awareness before you?

"What if you went through various phases of remembering, of increasing your awareness from gross ignorance of how things work to changing the system and then realizing there really is no system to change? Would you then begin to work on yourself? What if you recognized that you alone have the power to change your life? Would you change it or continue to live as you do?

"What if everything you ever believed was merely illusion and you resonated with being a soul, experiencing physicality in human form, over eons and eons of time? What if you knew it was all a game, of sorts, a way for souls to evolve, and perhaps even a way for souls to experience, express and expand the richness of *All That Is*. Would you continue to spend your energy creating things keeping you in limitation or would you change the game??

"Some of us changed the game and now focus on spreading Love and Light throughout all space and time. Some patiently, or not, strive to keep the Host of Oneness pure in body and mind to morph back to what we believe is our original form, pure, unlimited, unadulterated Light. These are the initiates of Oneness and this is but one of many places that they gather to live in the Light of One."

Life sure is getting interesting!

✡

Recircuiting Neural Pathways

An ongoing practice of the past few years certainly makes life interesting. I cannot imagine living as I do while going though what appears to be a massive body/mind change. Although sleeping habits remain erratic, I now sleep more throughout the night but often nap two hours after rising. Today, after eating breakfast, I give in to the demanding urge to nap. This occurs after days of restless sleep, and limited bowel activity (leading to the peak of the full moon) and two days of rather good sleep and loose stools.

While napping, spurts of wakefulness occur several times after conscious awareness clues me into ongoing guidance. I'm finally able to grab the pen and paper to document a message after ninety minutes.

"Recircuiting, of the neural pathways, now occurs as those of you ready to move forward listen to the Voice within. You are on a new journey of discovery as these changes take place so be sure to listen to your body. You will often feel the desire to rest, to incorporate these changes, as your Mother Earth changes as well.

"Let nothing dissuade you from the purpose your soul chose as this body's mission. Yes, some know the bottom line, as you refer to it (all is illusion as we are really figments of *All That Is* expressing soul's whims and desires in physical form), but recall whilst still in physical form you are serving the Host of One as agreed to before birth. Those not yet aware will soon be awakened to this truth as necessary changes take place upon your earth. Continue to listen to the Voice within as all move forward on the scale of evolution.

"We are the White Winged Consciousness of Nine (yes, another part of the grand illusion) ready to assist you."

✡

Relish in the Truth of Oneness

Today is the first day I consciously begin to take time to channel. A message comes within a minute of acknowledging my readiness.

"Be it known on all levels of existence there is no separation in any form. The separation you see in your physical world is but illusion of the small mind of one. Some members of society have learned to see through this illusion of darkness versus Light to show the way to others.

"Your being is one of the Love and Light of *All That Is*, perfect in every sense and never alone. Relish in this truth in coming days as the small mind of one fights with itself to regain control over the forces of what many refer to as separation. Yet know, in your small mind of one, all is illusion, a part of your own small mind of one, seeking recognition to regain the Wholeness of Self in all aspects. Not all levels of humanity are yet ready to seek this Truth of Self but each plays an important role in the process of knowing Self to the fullest degree.

"In coming days, you shall see many changes on your earth. Many shall seem to suffer consequences of their own making, and some will seem to suffer the consequences of ill thought upon others. Remember, all is in the small mind of one and judge not. Stay within your own thought, action and purpose to weather the coming years with dignity and awareness of Self."

✡

Review Thoughts and Feelings

It is quite easy to admit that I still forget to listen for messages. Sometimes I think life would be too easy to manifest only good. But it certainly is rewarding when what many would call small miracles occur.

Today is Monday and my Canadian friend will sail on a cruise with me in five days. I just completed the final draft of *Manifesting, Lightworker's Log* (Book 4) after working on it over the past three years. Of course, I wanted to get it into print even knowing changes will occur. Since I work most of the time, I wanted to take my work with me on the cruise. But it often takes at least two weeks for me to format a book, get it online, approved, ordered, printed and shipped. This time the process took less than 48 hours and the book proof is on its way to me. There's no doubt that it will arrive before we board!

Days continue to fill with naps between food, work and a bit of social activity. Intuition guided me to walk on the beach near sunset. After noticing light in my peripheral vision upon returning, it occurred to me to turn on the computer and listen. The following message came though immediately.

"The task before you now is one of bringing in the fold of One, never one aspect but all, as a Whole, to relish in the Light of One. Be clear in all the actions you take for each bears its own consequences. You must be aware of thoughts and feelings more sensibly

113

as these days move further into chaos, consciously reviewing each before deciding whether to take back the thought or feeling. This is done easily by repeating, 'I take back all ill thoughts and feelings not of Wholeness and Truth. I serve only the greater good of humanity with all thoughts, words, actions, and deeds.'

"Knowingly on the path of Oneness takes one further into the realm of *All That Is*, that place of perfection in all things. Know that as humanity moves through this purging process many will fall by the wayside, so to speak. Do not be concerned but know it is their soul's path to fully feel darkness and return gifts of experience to the Whole of *All That Is*.

"Take care in the days ahead and know you are one of many, watched over very carefully by your brothers and sisters of Light. We are in fact, each of you, on other realms of space, many without the complexities of time.

"I am Amanda here to serve as all coalesce into the Oneness in all aspects."

✡

Rewiring the Physical Frame

As ears itch throughout the night, and various body aches and pains make themselves known, it's clear that the process of rewiring physicality is not easy to move through as a human. We are changing the physical frame to be more in tune with the Lightbody left so long ago as souls. This process will take many years but it has begun in earnest for many lightworkers, wayshowers, and starseeds.

Old systems continue to fall away and as they do, it's often difficult to let go of these time-worn habits of thinking everything through. I am of the mindset that there really are no levels of any sort for all here is illusion. This mindset doesn't seem to help when intestinal distress or unusual headaches appear suddenly but it is a strong belief honed through years of studying *A Course in Miracles* and living through various experiences.

So what are we to do to motor through this illusion? Shall we stay in our head and continue to try and perfect? Shall we continue to give up our power to follow others who believe they know the way through physical life? Or shall we listen to the Voice within and go with what resonates? Is it possible to participate within group settings, where focus seems in keeping one in a physical form, without seeming to be separate in mind and body? Can we not focus on what this physical frame is experiencing without calling in the teachings of others in the illusion? Can we focus on the possibility that body changes may just be a sign of morphing back to a form left long ago rather than trying to figure out how our emotions cause this state of being?

"Ego resists. Spirit lives on."

The bottom line is that it's now necessary to connect with others seeming to be separate and, in the process, find ways to interact without moving out of the heart space, regardless of surrounding experience. There are three important things to do at this time.

- Care for the physical host.

- Shine forth the Light throughout all realms of space and time (and as you spread that Light, relish in the wonderful feeling of Oneness).

- Form local communities of Love and Light.

Common signs of the rewire process include odd sleeping hours; exhaustion; incessant, upper body heat; hot feet; itchy ears; headaches; various body aches and pains; intestinal distress; and ear ringing. We must deal with these physical signs in the best way possible to move though this process with ease and grace. Search the Internet for helpful advice and visit these website pages: http://www.LightworkersLog.com/page85.html and http://www.LightworkersLog.com/page52.html. Helpful suggestions and signs of ascension are also in *Bits of Wisdom* by SAM available through New Leaf Distributing, CreateSpace at http://www.createspace.com/3947503   and Amazon.

Lightworker's Log offers a wealth of ascension resources, such as articles, podcasts videos, and various links to more tools. Visit http://www.LightworkersLog.com/revsam/page5.html to balance the scale of giving and receiving.

✡

Streaming Light

Checking the amount of Light within body cells has become somewhat of a practice for me. And yet, it seems especially difficult to do today as I try at dawn. A message comes as I ponder over this dilemma.

"Begin by focusing on the Light within your body. Take in more golden Light from the top of your head if you feel more is necessary. Now begin to allow this Light to flow more rapidly, like sparks or dots bumping around in a contained space. Allow the dots of Light to expand and move through your physical frame to the emotional body. Feel the exquisite joy of a body in great pleasure as the dots of Light permeate this body. Allow the Light to now congeal into one massive flow of Light energy as it continues to expand outside the physical/emotional body to the space beyond, the ethereal form encasing your Essence. "Continue to envision this Light moving in a fluid manner to encompass all space around you. Expand your field of Light to cover the room, the space in which you exist, the city, the state, and country of existence. Now move beyond this space to stream your unique flow of Light meeting other flows of unique Light to encompass all space and time. Picture the flow of Light no longer a flow but a permanent Light, which covers everything, every space, every time, and continues without end.

"When you are ready to return to your physical existence, begin to move your fingers and toes to reconnect with the physical body. Open your eyes and end the Light Spreading Session with the Love and Joy that you are.

"We are the White-Winged Consciousness of Nine here to help all realize the true form of Nature. Thank you for your assistance."

It's clear when the message ends that this is to be recorded onto a CD, for personal use, and to share with others. Since I'm still in the process of formatting *Book of One :-) Volume 3*, there's still room to add it to the draft.

Please note: Those not familiar with the practice of building a body of light may find "Lightbody Expansion" in *Book of One :-) Volume 2* helpful.

✡

Think Life-Affirming Thoughts

"Once you change your memory your perception changes. Let's expand upon that, shall we?

"Your physical brain holds all memories of this life. Your ethereal brain, if you will, holds all memories of past lives. Your two brains then help you to motor through this illusion called life. When you change your thinking in the realm in which you exist, for instance the earth realm, you then can make new decisions to change your experience. As you sleep, you visit other realms of earth life and other realms of your soul's existence. Changing the way you think in this realm, changes the way you also think on those other realms.

"So do you see how conducting your life differently helps? Do you see how filling your daily life, your brain, with life-affirming thoughts and deeds, rather than fear and limitation, helps?

"We shall help humanity make this change together as One. Stay tuned to the higher realms of ethereal existence to remain in your heart. Keep thoughts pure, on life-affirming activities to ride the wave of freedom that now knocks upon your door. Thank you for your help on this and other realms."

"We are the Keeper of One."

In this realm of existence the purging and cleansing of mass consciousness continues with reports of additional massive earth changes. I am reminded of the work and preparation, to help humanity and my soul, over the last eight to ten years, which led me to this point in time and space. These past several years have been tumultuous, as with many other lightworkers, having rid myself of memories, physical belongings, family, friends and anything else that affects higher good. I have moved more times than I care to count but am always where I need to be. I now reside in Fort Lauderdale, Florida in a very high energy spot.

I cannot stress enough the need to feel emotions and to release negative ones in life-affirming ways. Remember, we must feel the feelings of human life to move forward in thinking to a state of Oneness. For it is only when we put ourselves in someone else's shoes, or see ourselves through the eyes of another, that we have more knowledge to change awareness and therefore our experience.

The "Lightworker's Log Book Series" documents a changing field of awareness from very, very out of touch, with what many call God, to communicating on a daily basis and guiding others. Books reach different states of awareness and those in the "Lightworker's Log Book Series" raise ones vibrational rate. There are also many free articles, book excerpts, audio files and videos on the Lightworker's Log Web site (http://www.LightworkersLog.com). There's also a free "True Vision Sample CD" that accompanies the book *Prayer Treatments: Lightworker's Log*, when purchased through me. An audio version of *Book of One :-) Volume*

1 is in the making. These tools helped me a great deal and listening to them can help you as well.

To order *Prayer Treatments: Lightworker's Log* along with the free "True Vision Sample CD" mail $14 to SAM at P.O. Box 39385, Fort Lauderdale, FL, 33339-9385.

✡

Walk the Talk

A message comes at dawn.

"It's not about making money anymore. It's time to walk the talk, to join WE Consciousness fully by expressing the Oneness of Life and allowing it to come through us. We must trust that Source, the Universe, whatever we refer to as God will care for our needs, fully and completely.

"This is the time of all times, the time of coming together, as One. Many of us feel this now as others fall into the fray of forgetting. Do not let the massive energies pull you back into the black abyss of nothingness but choose to create new boundaries where there is absolutely no limits whatsoever. You do this by following your heart, going with what resonates for you, what gives you joy, what fills you with that knowing that you are indeed part of something much larger than your self.

"You must enter this consciousness fully now to weather coming energies. They will be massive, bringing many people to their knees, so to speak, bringing many to the breaking point, as they forget their True Self. You as a lightworker, as a worker of the new energies, must maintain your sense of Oneness to help those ready to move forward on the path of remembrance. Let nothing dissuade you from your task for it is in your own consciousness that you shall enter and live in the New World.

"We have come to you this day to break fully all old habits of limitation, your self-

123

imposed limitations. It is time for you to recognize that there is only Love, Light, Life and you are truly That of what it is.

"We are the Keeper of One."

I immediately got the point since lately I've been adamant about including my Amazon book link with every post. It is now time to trust that Source will fully support me without any kind of advertising on Facebook posts. After putting quotes of Oneness on beautiful pictures I then connected to Facebook, posted them without any kind of book advertising, and fell back asleep.

✡

World Roller Coaster Ride

"The disease you feel is, as you know, part of the purging process of humanity. You are taking on the thoughts of others in the matrix of illusion, and feeling your feelings as well, but at this time feelings are rampant on earth. So what are you specifically to do? Stay in your heart space. Trust that all will continue to be well. Continue to watch for the signs of change and follow the synchronicities to get to where you always need to be to stay out of the sway of ongoing drama.

"This world will continue to get much worse, or so it shall seem but for those remaining in the heart, all will remain well within the reach of Nirvana. Energies, as you know, remain erratic. Take care of your physical host and believe what you feel, what you sense, what you know as truth. Nothing shall remain the same, not your body, not your world, and certainly not your state of mind. Welcome to the world roller coaster ride of surprise, delight, and love, as all else passes away.

"We are ever near waiting for your response. We are the energies of One."

This message was very difficult to type and I kept misspelling words even while looking at the keyboard to type, because the words came so quickly.

✡

~ Part Three ~

Affirmations

"I create greater and greater states of abundance based on my gifts and talents."

♥

"With ease and grace, I fully accept all downloads to help with humanity's evolution."

♥

"Everyday I am more aware of the greater aspects of Self. And I am ever grateful for this Truth."

♥

"I draw forth the Power of One to guide me through this day for I AM the Power, the Truth, the Beauty, the Love of *All That Is*, perfect, Whole and free."

♥

"I AM moving toward a more joyful, fulfilling life, taking more chances to see where they lead. There is no right or wrong. There is only experience and I can choose the experiences that resonate for me. I can be more spontaneous again."

♥

"I AM a lighthouse beacon radiating the Light of
One for all to enter."

♥

"I AM Perfect, Whole and Free and it is all I will ever be!"

♥

"I AM that of which *It* is, Perfect, Whole, and True."

♥

"I AM perfection, Perfect, Whole and Free and I spread that Light to the grid of humanity."

♥

About the Author

SAM, author of the "Lightworker's Log Book Series," is an ordained minister, channel of higher realms, teacher, founder of SAM, I AM Productions, assisting clients to help others find the Divine Spark within, and administrator of the popular Internet resource, Lightworker's Log (LightworkersLog.com). Spreading Spirit's message of Oneness throughout the globe, SAM is a wayshower helping others to learn the truth of BEing so humanity can return unique figments back to *All That Is*.

The Lightworker's Log Book Series

Book One: Death of the Sun

Book Two: A Change in Perception

Lightworker's Log :-) Transformation

Manifesting: Lightworker's Log

Prayer Treatments: Lightworker's Log

Adventures in Greece and Turkey

Earth Angels

Return to Light: John of God Helps

Bits of Wisdom

Book of One :-) Volume 1

Book of One :-) Volume 2

Book of One :-) Volume 3

www.ingramcontent.com/pod-product-compliance
Lightning Source LLC
LaVergne TN
LVHW011239080426

835509LV00005B/558